RELAXATION & MEDITATION

ENCHANTED FLOWERS

MANDALA AND FLORAL PATTERNS

COLORING BOOK FOR ADULTS

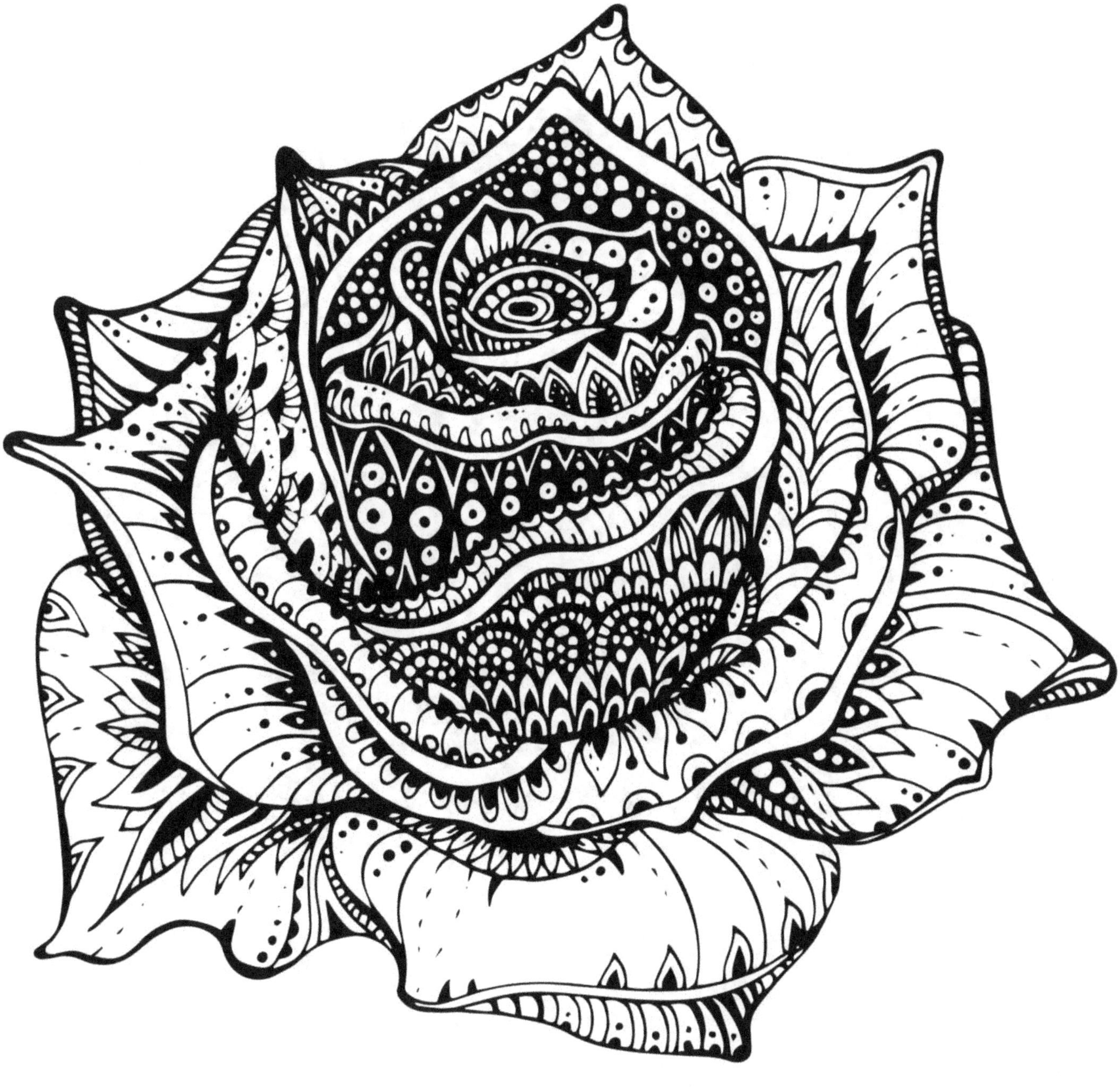

www.ingramcontent.com/pod-product-compliance
Lightning Source LLC
Chambersburg PA
CBHW081156280526
45787CB00008B/3352
9781548449582